HEADLINE

a beginner's guide to mastering the media

David Arscott

Pomegranate

Practicals

*"Tell you everything you need to know
- and leave out everything you don't"*

Copyright © David Arscott, 1998
No part of this publication may be reproduced without permission.

David Arscott is a writer and broadcaster. He has worked as a
journalist for local and national newspapers, and as a radio
producer and presenter for the BBC.

British Library Cataloguing-in-Publication Data.
A catalogue record for this book is available from the British Library.

ISBN 0 9519876 7 4

Published by Pomegranate Press,
Church Cottage, Westmeston, Hassocks, Sussex BN6 8RH
Telephone/fax: 01273 846743
E-mail: 106461.1316@compuserve. com

Printed in England by M.D. Morgan, Red Lake Terrace, Ore,
Hastings, Sussex.

So who needs a headline?

You do! If you hadn't at least considered using the media for some advantageous publicity it's a fair bet that you wouldn't have taken this book off the shelf.

And unless you're some kind of a recluse, it's equally likely that you're involved with at least one organisation which, for whatever reason, occasionally has something to tell the world at large.

Yet however much we appreciate the value of media exposure, most of us would run a mile before thinking of making an approach to our local newspaper, radio or television station. This is to miss a great opportunity.

If you're among the reticent majority, don't worry: HEADLINE has been devised with the shy and retiring in mind!

This isn't a book for the would-be superstar (although it's as good a place to start as any), but for ordinary men and women with a message to put across - publicity secretaries, events organisers, campaigners, protesters, the owners of small businesses with a product to promote.

Our easy-to-digest 'tips & wrinkles' explain the way the media works, outline the essentials of a good story, show you how to write a compelling press release, prepare you for your first interview - and then put what you've learned to the test.

And we've an accompanying audio tape *(see page 26)* which is full of practical tips about being interviewed 'live' on your local radio station.

With the steady proliferation of local and community stations to complement a wide range of free and 'paid for' local papers, there have never been more outlets eager to welcome anyone with a story to tell. And, as HEADLINE demonstrates, it really isn't difficult to become one of those storytellers yourself.

Go on: master the media!

Newsbreaks . . .

This little exercise will eventually give you an idea of how much you've learned. Take a glance at the six posers below, then come back to them once you've absorbed everything in the book. We offer our own solutions on page 30.

Newsbreak 1

You run a thriving export business, and at one of your busiest times of the year a local radio reporter rings up to ask for your views on the Government's new tax proposals. You feel like wringing his unlovely neck - but how should you react?

Newsbreak 2

You're involved with a charity, and you're asked whether you can mange to fix some publicity for a new fund-raising drive. Your sister says her husband's best friend knows a lively reporter on the local television station and that she can put you in touch with him. What's your next move?

Newsbreak 3

The local council is about to evict you from your home. You decide to write to the media in a last-ditch effort to save your way of life. It is, however, a complex story, which really needs pages of detailed explanation. Where do you begin?

Newsbreak 4

You've organised a chess tournament for several years without any media interest. This year a brilliant six-year-old girl has entered and may well beat a grand master. Suddenly the media are extremely interested. But you want to maintain the dignity of your tournament. How do you balance things?

Newsbreak 5

During a radio interview the conversation about the award-winning pub which you manage seems to be drifting towards the evils of alcohol in drink-driving cases. This diversion, not surprisingly, makes you very angry. What do you do?

Newsbreak 6

When the television company asks for an interview with someone from your sailing club you know the Commodore will be furious if he's not the spokesman. You also happen to know that he's extremely boring and has a tendency to strike ridiculous poses for the camera. What's the best option?

The devil you know

*Few people have a good word to say
for reporters, but - like it or not -
they're the folk aspiring headline-
hunters have to deal with . . .*

It's not our business in these pages to defend everything that journalists get up to - and we'd be the last to claim that those who deal with them never have good reason to complain about the treatment they suffer.

But the first HEADLINE lesson can't be repeated often enough: Since you can't single-handedly change the way the media works, you'll simply have to adjust to its peculiarities if you're to succeed in winning those valuable column inches and precious minutes of airtime.

Here's our 12-point guide to the mindset of your average 'hack', which we present in abbreviated form on the next page. By 'he' we mean, of course, 'he or she': the reporter you meet is as likely to be a woman as a man:

1 He's out to get a good story, not to get YOU.
Ignore this paragraph if you're an embezzler, child molester or serial killer, in which case you *can* expect to get the full treatment, and deservedly so. Otherwise, beware of taking a reporter's enquiry as if it constitutes a personal attack, since this may *a.* immediately sour your relationship with him and *b.* stop you thinking clearly about how to react.

The reverse applies, of course. He may give you great coverage, but don't let that fool you into believing that he's for ever on your side. The *story* is what he's after.

2 He thrives on the unusual.
There are those who complain that although hundreds of planes a day take off from their local airport, the journalist is interested only in the one that crashes. To which the answer is that news bulletins would be pretty boring otherwise. Yes, good news can be rivetting, too - the captain saved hundreds of lives by managing to land the plane safely on one wheel - but, unless it's simply too important to ignore, it must be *different.*

3

Meet the reporter
- the Headline
12 point guide

1   He/she is out to get a good story, not to get YOU
2   He thrives on the unusual
3   He jumps to conclusions
4   He's ignorant
5   He has deadlines to meet
6   He thinks in headlines
7   He's often desperate for a story
8   But he's wary of accepting what you tell him at face value
9   He's trained to be impartial
10 He's persistent
11 But he can suddenly lose interest in favour of another story
12 He's human

3 He jumps to conclusions.

Time is precious, and the reporter needs to make sense of what may be quite a complicated story. Try to imagine how the facts look from his point of view and you've a good chance of preventing mistakes before they happen.

4 He's ignorant.

This isn't the gratuitous insult that it seems, but a warning to you that the reporter can't be expected to possess an intimate knowledge of the way you or your organisation work.

In reality, journalists tend to have a far better than average awareness of the way the world goes about its business, but it's easy to imagine from all those searching questions that he knows far more than he does.

The world is awash with rueful interviewees who bemoan the fact that reporters 'always get it wrong'. Just count the number of facts in an average story, and you'll quickly realise that most of them get a very large percentage of them right most of the time. That's perhaps little comfort if a painful mistake has been made, but take some of the responsibility upon yourself. Make sure that you spell out the important facts to him - without, of course, managing to suggest that he's a complete idiot.

5 He has deadlines to meet.

If the story's a big one, the reporter will wait for it as long as he has to, but a lesser yarn may not survive the next deadline - especially on a weekly paper, where a further seven days will make your chestnut decidedly hoary.

If you're genuinely not sufficiently prepared when he makes his call, make sure that you don't lose his interest. Tell him when he *can* talk to you, and make sure that he has all the telephone numbers he may need. If you sense that he's already growing cool and you really do need that publicity, try to overcome your own reservations as best you can.

6 He thinks in headlines.

Yes, of course some stories are far too complex to be satisfactorily summed up in a witty catchline, but most fit into a number of familiar patterns. One (crude) test of a striking tale is whether you can encapsulate it in a few words to your husband/wife/lover/friend the moment you meet: *Mary's left Mark for a choirboy*, you might say. Or *I've won the lottery with my very*

> *"There is much to be said in favour of modern journalism. By giving us the opinions of the uneducated, it keeps us in touch with the ignorance of the community."*
> Oscar Wilde

first ticket! Or *The dog's just been run over by a bus.*

If this suggests a triviality of mind on the part of the journalist, we should stress that there's room in the more serious news outlets for detailed investigations which patiently sift through complicated facts. The reporter nevertheless still needs to see the story in his mind's eye at the outset. What's the gist of it? Can he explain it to his editor in that one-line manner? To attract him in the first place, you need to be able to pare your own story to the bone. Think clearly about what you want to say.

7 He's often desperate for a story.
All those newspaper pages, all those hours of airtime, have to be filled on a regular basis, and there are times when journalists begin to despair of finding enough material. You may just be able to supply the vital item, so don't make the mistake of being lukewarm about your own story. Feed his need!

8 But he's wary of accepting what you tell him at face value.
A damn nerve, you may feel, when the persistent reporter hammers away at your version of events. But try to imagine what his life is like: people are always trying to shoot him a line. It's his duty to check everything out - and to have a healthy suspicion about motives. So don't get rattled, but give him the evidence he needs.

9 He's trained to be impartial.
If you're involved in a controversy, it's probably clear to you that your opponents are no-good rogues and

---

Read - and hear - all about it . . .

You've much more chance of making an impact in the media if you actually read it, listen to it and watch it. If that's not your habit, but you have a story to tell, try to make up for lost time. Buy a copy; tune in.

Newspaper styles and their news values are influenced by their format (tabloid or broadsheet); by the social profile of the area they serve; and by the priorities of the editor. Get to know what's what in your patch. Take aim!

charlatans, but you can't expect the reporter to share your opinions. He *may* eventually come round to your point of view, but he knows that if he's seduced by one party (perhaps because he takes to the individual or shares similar prejudices) he runs the danger of making a serious error of judgement. He's trained to be cool, and you shouldn't attempt to enrol him in your cause.

10 He's persistent.
A good story to a journalist is like a bone to a dog - at least while there's still meat attached to it. He'll probably want to check his facts more than once, so don't imagine that you can simply send him a press release and not expect to be bothered by a telephone call. If you want your story used, you'll just have to accept that you may be pursued for days on end. That's part of the price you have to pay for getting involved.

11 But he can suddenly lose interest in favour of another story.
Reporters tend to have fairly short attention spans, and they often get very excited about stories which can suddenly seem not worth chasing up after all. This is useful to know, because you may easily become lulled into a false sense of security by his initial eagerness. If

that encourages you to be offhand with him (perhaps asking him to ring back tomorrow, after you've had your hair cut/car serviced/dog shampooed) beware: he may not ring back after all. There's always another, more gripping, story out there waiting to break.

12 He's human.
Which means that you have to have a relationship with him, however brief and superficial. Reporters are an informal breed and dislike bumptious officialdom and stuffed-shirts of all kinds. Don't put on airs and graces with them.

The better you get on with people, the more chance you have of mastering the media. If this is your weakness, work on it.

Blame the subs!
If the newspaper coverage of your story includes a sensational or punning headline which appals you, don't leap for the reporter's throat. He doesn't put the paper together. That's the job of the sub editors (or subs), who may also rewrite some of his copy.

Blaming the subs is a convenient get out for him, of course - but sometimes it's a justifiable defence.

The perils of 'No comment'

It's commonly believed that a terse 'No comment' is the wisest response to an unwanted enquiry from a journalist. Don't believe it!

We'd like to think that most of your dealings with the local media will be painless and friendly - and, indeed, even positively profitable once you've mastered the lessons in this book! - but there may come a time when you're asked a question you'd rather not answer.

Let's imagine that you're a youth club leader and that a few local residents have complained about the noise that your young charges make of an evening. That 'No comment' reply of yours may be all that the reporter needs to convince himself (and his editor) that he's covered both sides of the question.

When you open your newspaper you find all kinds of unfair and inflammatory remarks about your wonderful youth club, with a pathetic 'No comment' from you at the end.

Just think how that will be interpreted!

No, since you can't prevent the story coming out (you're not being accused of anything criminal, after all) you must work hard to have it told your way.

If you're unprepared for the question when it comes, tell the reporter that you (or someone else) will call back within a certain time - allowing for his deadline. Make sure you honour this promise. And make sure, too, that you have something to say which will swing sympathy your way.

The potential headline NOISY KIDS TERRORISE NEIGHBOURHOOD could, with a little shrewdness on your part, become the far preferable NEIGHBOURHOOD MEANIES THREATEN YOUNGSTERS' FUN.

Recognising a newsworthy story comes with practice, but if you're after publicity it's worth taking a step back and trying to see things with a reporter's eye. He thrives on the unusual, remember . . .

A GOOD STORY

We well remember the day that a conference-load of environmental health officers tried to get to grips with what to many of them was a highly dangerous business: learning to cope with the demands of the media.

After a session in which they were given the kind of basic grounding that this book provides (and during which most of them had seemed very receptive), they were invited to take part in a 'mock' interview for the local radio station. What, we asked, was the big news in their world at the moment?

By way of answer out came a thick and heavy volume which turned out to be some new legislation on various aspects of environmental health.

It didn't, as you might expect, make gripping reading, but we found a paragraph or two about a law which would give workers the right to

---

"News is what a chap who doesn't care much about anything wants to read. And it's only news until he's read it. After that it's dead."

Evelyn Waugh, 'Scoop'

---

prevent colleagues who smoked from lighting up their cigarettes in the workplace. Good human interest stuff, and we duly ran an interview with a volunteer 'spokesman'.

Afterwards the floor was thrown open for discussion. How much had they learned?

The answer, in a few cases, was very little indeed. For a handful of the audience took issue with the trivial nature of the interview - not because of the questions asked, but because this topic had been chosen at all.

Couldn't we see that there were more serious matters in this legislation, covering vital issues such as staff training, weights and measures or food wrapping?

We had to begin all over again with those ten points about the typical reporter, to which the cry went up: 'But why should journalists behave like that?'

Why does the sun come up in the morning? If you're going to chase those headlines, however small, you just have to accept the fact that journalists are on the lookout for interesting stories.

Their idea of exactly what is interesting will vary, of course (and a reporter writing for a specialist health magazine might well seize upon the 'serious' points those conference delegates wanted covered), but

Coming up roses - a true tale

Doreen K. was organising her village flower show. A week before the great event she found to her horror that someone had removed all her carefully placed roadside signs.

Having rung the police, she learned that the culprits were none other than the county council, who had 'cleaned up' the verges for many miles around.

It was the weekend, and Doreen could only leave an angry message on the council's answerphone. But she went one better, by ringing her local television station. Did they know what was going on? They didn't, and they were keen to run the story.

On the Monday morning, just as the camera crew was due to arrive, Doreen had a telephone call from a council spokesman, who explained that there had been a blitz on the posting of unauthorised signs, but that he was prepared to make an exception in her case.

This was a dead story, Doreen imagined -

and she dutifully rang the television station.

Not so, however. The council's policy WAS a story, and Doreen's temporary plight made a good 'photo' opportunity. She was filmed first in front of an empty verge and then in the process of carrying the signs from the council depot back to where they belonged. Her local newspaper followed the story up, with a half-page splash.

'We had a record turnout on Saturday,' she laughed afterwards. 'I'm sure the publicity brought more people in.'

you have to allow for their appetite for the new, the only, the strange and the striking.

Sometimes a story will come to meet you, and then *(see opposite)* you must grab hold of it before it disappears.

More often, though, you'll know what you're after, but you won't have a clue about how to interest the media in your project. You can't see the story, in other words.

Don't lose heart!

Let's imagine that you've been given the job of increasing the membership of your local Afternoon Club, which meets in the church hall every other week, with an occasional speaker, a raffle and a cup of tea. Nothing interesting about that, quite frankly. It might merit a line in a local 'paper of record' (the sort that includes just about everything), but

otherwise you're likely to draw a complete blank.

But take a close look at the membership. Is it very old? That might not sound very promising, but you could work out the

> **"Perhaps if I wanted to be understood or to understand I would bamboozle myself into belief, but I am a reporter; God exists only for leader-writers."**
> **Graham Greene, 'The Quiet American'**

average age and write a press release on the lines of: *Mallingham's Afternoon Club is thought to have the oldest membership in the county,* explaining that you're after new, younger blood - and tempting both your local paper and the television station to take pictures of your golden oldies. (Do warn everyone first!)

Or look at the range

of your members' working experience. If it makes a rather impressive list, take this as your theme, adding that you're now looking for a brain surgeon, a belly dancer and a snake charmer to complete the set.

The basic story is the same, but you've found the journalist an unusual 'angle' from which to approach it.

Our sample press releases and matching 'Headline hints' will give you a few more ideas of this kind.

You may even find that story-telling is fun!

11

12

THE PRESS RELEASE

Don't make the beginner's mistake of believing that the media are bound to hear about your activities through some handy celestial grapevine. They need to be told . . .

A great many fine trees are felled in vain to produce the vast flood of material which engulfs a news editor's desk.

The moral is that your press release has to be special in order to be noticed.

What you have to say is obviously important (to you, at least), but it's vital that you present it in a way which gives it a chance of being plucked from that swirling tide.

We give you some examples on the next few pages, but here are the main points to bear in mind:

Use a word processor or typewriter. Your copy should be easy to read. If you *must* use a pen, don't scrawl.

Use only one sheet of paper, and write on one side of it. Your journalist, remember, is short of both time and patience.

Tell your story simply and in short sentences. Don't use jargon: it will get in the way of what you have to say.

Give the names and telephone numbers of all the relevant contacts. The reporter may lose interest if he can't quickly find someone to talk to.

Be available. It's no use sending out a press release just as you're about to go away on holiday.

Whose desk should it land on?

It's a great advantage in seeking publicity to know something about the media you're likely to approach.

Keep an eye open for regular by-lines in the newspaper. Is there one particular reporter who regularly deals with the kind of material you're offering?

This first-hand knowledge may well suggest the obvious recipient of your press release. Otherwise, address it to the news editor.

A

Yak Cheese is New Delicacy

Cheese made from yak's milk in the mountains of Tibet is just one of an unusual range of products at a new shop in Paddlecombe's High Street.

Proprietors John and Jane Anklehorn have travelled the world to find exotic varieties to sell in The Cheese Shop.

Says Jane: 'Cheddar and Brie are good cheeses, but we wanted to find new tastes for jaded palates. Just imagine serving your guests smoked llama cheese from Peru!'

The Cheese Shop is at 149 High Street, Paddlecombe.

Telephone: Shop   Paddlecombe 3192
                       Home   Paddlecombe 2477

N.B. You are invited to send a reporter to sample our new cheeses (and enjoy a glass of wine) on Thursday March 9, from 4 to 7pm.

It's a good idea to give the press release a title, but you needn't try too hard to be a headline writer. That's their job.

Note, first, the simplicity of the sentences. Don't overstretch yourself with complicated chains of thought that can't be contained within twenty words at a time.

Next note the 'jaded palates' phrase. It suggests that you'll come up with some good comments when the reporters gets in touch. And if the paper is lazy and doesn't make contact at all, at least it has a built-in comment to enliven its text.

And note, finally, that temptation at the foot of the press release. The early timing should attract reporters who have better things to do in the evening, but who will be very happy to fit your event into their working day.

You must be prepared, of course, for requests for others times to visit in order to satisfy particular deadlines (and they won't expect the wine if they come then), but you've practically assured yourself of publicity now. Journalists, like most of us, love a little pampering.

This is a good example of making the best of what might at first seem a pretty difficult job.

There's nothing 'sexy' about driving people to hospital, but the hint of crisis ('shan't be able to cope') is always alluring to a reporter. Note, too, the 80,000 miles old Fred has driven: reporters like dramatic global figures, so it's often worthwhile doing your sums.

Riding with a volunteer may not offer a white-knuckle experience (though who knows!), but there are good picture opportunities here for newspapers and television, plus sound - door slams, key in ignition, driver talks over purr of engine etc - for local radio.

One contact number is usually enough, but in this case it was thought that the reporter might wish to get in touch with the hospital administrator himself. If you DO give several numbers, make sure that anyone approached lets the others know.

B

Hospital Drivers Needed

Frisdon General Hospital is running short of volunteer drivers to take patients from their homes to the hospital and back again.

Says the chairman of the League of Hospital Friends, Mrs Dorothy Jones: 'These people do vital work for the community, but they are often elderly folk themselves and can only work so many hours a week.

'We need more volunteers, and preferably young ones, or we shan't be able to cope.'

Volunteers are paid for their petrol, and most give their services for a few hours each week.

The longest-serving volunteer, Fred Jackson, calculates that he has driven nearly 80,000 miles during the past 20 years.

Anyone wishing to volunteer should contact the hospital secretary on Frisdon 4398.

Contacts: Mrs Lee Jones, Chairman, League of Hospital Friends: Frisdon 7323

Charles Gordon, Unit Administrator, Frisdon General: Frisdon 4398 extension 66

Reporters are invited to accompany one of the drivers on a hospital run. Please contact Mrs Jones or the hospital secretary.

C

Busy Scouts Hit 20-Activity Target

A new climbing course and a canoeing trip to the Wye Valley will give New Town Venture Scouts the opportunity of trying twenty different events this year.

'We've been increasing our activities every year,' says Scout leader John Rankin, 'and we've had the round 20 in our sights for some time.

'Apart from the usual camping and hiking, we find our young men and women a wide range of exciting and unusual things to do.

'And we get many of our best ideas from the Venture Scouts themselves.'

Recruiting for the new season has just begun, and outgoing and adventurous young people between the ages of 16 and 18 should turn up at the scout hut in Langport Road on any of the next three Thursdays or contact John Rankin any evening on New Town 6313.

REPORTERS ARE INVITED TO WATCH OUR VENTURE SCOUTS ABSEILING FROM THE ROOF OF THE ALLIANCE & LEICESTER BUILDING IN NEW TOWN HIGH STREET THIS TUESDAY LUNCHTIME AT 1PM.

John Rankin's telephone numbers:
    Daytime New Town 4444
    Evening New Town 6313

All organisations need the occasional membership drive, and the trick is to make them as interesting as possible. These Venture Scouts may not be doing very much more this year than last, but the 20-activity target is a good angle. You don't need to name them all (though you should have the list ready for the more fastidious kind of reporter). Keep your press releases short and to the point.

Note the two telephone numbers at the foot of the press release. You don't want new recruits bothering you at your workplace, but it's important that the media should be able to reach you at any time. (They can quickly lose interest, remember).

The abseiling stunt, or something similar, should attract most of the media, depending upon what else is going on at the time. The local paper may send only a photographer, since they already have the press release and will have spoken to you beforehand. Make sure that he has the details of the people he's photographed: it's not a bad idea to give him (very short) backgrounds on Venture Scouts who've done interesting things: 'Mandy Watson is a first year drama student at Loughborough University and has climbed several of the smaller Himalayan peaks during the past three years.'

The paper may run the event as a picture story, in which the caption does all the work, and the photographer may write it himself, so give him a spare copy of your press release and stress the recruitment drive and the telephone number. If he seems at all vague, ring your newsroom contact and - in a friendly way, of course - stress that you're hoping for that vital information to be included.

| Headline hints | D |

The plan here is to get advance publicity for your AGM, not necessarily to get a reporter along to it (though that would be a nice bonus).

The 'figures to be released' ploy is simply a way of tying the story to the meeting. Don't withhold those figures from a journalist who rings up to ask for them (news 'embargoes' are for special occasions between consenting parties), but do stress that there will be a more detailed report at the meeting.

Note that 'annual general meeting' has been typed without capital letters. A common curse of amateur (and some professional) press releases is the ugly capitalising of the first letter of any word the writer feels to be important. Fine in Germany, perhaps. Avoid it here.

* There's usually more than one angle you can find once you get the hang of things.

Can you think of another way of attracting the media, using the information used in press release D?

We've an alternative version on page 22.

D

Breast is Best in Botley

Figures to be released at the annual general meeting of the Botley branch of the Natural Childbirth Trust show a marked increase in the percentage of local women breastfeeding their babies.

Says branch chairman Sally Stewart: 'More than 60 per cent of mothers in our area are managing to breastfeed their babies for three months and more, which is a marked improvement on a few years ago.'

Breastfeeding counsellors will be at the AGM to advise mothers, intending mothers and their partners. Non-members are welcome.

The AGM is at the Hume Hall in Grove Road on Saturday September 3rd at 2.30pm.

Contact: Maria Holsworthy, Botley 2246

A question of timing

The timing of your press release isn't always crucial, but you do need to be aware of deadlines and 'silly seasons'.

A weekly paper published on a Friday may well have a Wednesday deadline. If you send something to them on Thursday, there's a good chance that they'll throw it away unless it's a first-class story: there's plenty of time before the next edition, isn't there? Better to get it to them at the beginning of the week.

And don't forget that papers can be very short of good material at holiday times, when everything slows down and many of their own staff are away. A good time to approach them, therefore.

As for local radio, good stories are often used up during the day, so that the poor overnight reporter is looking for fresh material with which to enliven the daybreak bulletin. Your story may not be sensational, but deliver your press release late in the day and you could well have a better chance of getting it used.

Watch out, on the other hand, for strong stories which will kill your own. If you know that there's a major murder trial or a royal visit which will dominate your local media tomorrow, far better to hold back story until all the fuss has died down.

Breast 'Milkmaids' Do the Rounds in Botley

A team of breast-feeding counsellors is visiting Botley to give practical advice to mothers of young babies.

They'll be at the annual meeting of the Natural Childbirth Trust at the Hume Hall, Grove Road, on Saturday September 3rd at 2.30pm.

Says the branch chairman, Sally Stewart: 'More than 60 per cent of mothers in our area are managing to breastfeed their babies for three months and more, which is a marked improvement on a few years ago.

'There can be difficulties in the early stages, which understandably puts some mothers off, but we've proved that with a little basic help most women are able to produce a good supply of milk for their babies.

'It's good for the babies and very rewarding for their mothers!'

The AGM is open to non-members - and, of course, to men as well as women.

NEW PRESS RELEASE D

(see p. 20)

Yes, this is better than the first version because it manages to tie the story inextricably to the meeting. And in stressing the counselling angle you have increased the chances of people coming along.

Don't worry if you can't think of a smart headline, but be aware that some lazy papers are only too happy to run an uncontroversial story much as it's given to them if it doesn't require much tweaking.

Remember the cardinal rules: find an angle; keep it simple; and keep it short.

'We've got your press release'

It's vital that you're fully prepared for stage two of the 'woo the media' operation. The reporter who calls you is interested, but he'll almost certainly want to know more.

What do you do when he rings? It's time to put a little more flesh on the bare bones of our 'The Devil You Know' guide:

He's out to get a good story, not to get YOU/trained to be impartial/wary of accepting what you tell him at face value. Be relaxed and cooperative with him, and don't try to dodge his questions.

If there's a controversial element to the story, you must expect him to play devil's advocate. He may even have the cheek to ask you for the name of someone who speaks for the 'opposition': it will be tempting to tell him to find one for himself, but do try to curb your anger. You want this story told, don't forget, and if he's half-way competent he won't run it without canvassing both sides.

When a reporter calls in response to your press release you can certainly congratulate yourself on a successful opening move. But don't overdose on pride - there's hard work still to be done . . .

He jumps to conclusions/He's ignorant. You may believe that your press release was the very model of clarity, but do be alert for possible misinterpretations. This is probably your one and only chance to get it right, so make sure he understands what you're saying.

He can suddenly lose interest in favour of another story. He may be searching for something a little stronger than is evident in your press release, and a muttered lack-lustre set of replies from you will soon persuade him to cut his losses and look elsewhere for his next headline. You need to be as persuasive as your press release evidently was.

He's human. So don't think of him as a bug-eyed monster. Chat. Smile. Relate!

23

Out of the blue

*You're the golf club
secretary and the
local newspaper
puts it to you that a
group of people have
been refused
membership
because of their low
social standing . . .
or you chair the
Women's Institute,
and a radio reporter
asks you to
comment on a
national survey
suggesting that the
organisation is
failing to attract
young business-
women . . . or you
run the allotments
committee, and your
local television
wants to film you,
at the plot of their
choice, responding
to criticism that
your members are
turning the area
into an eyesore with
their corrugated
iron sheds and
weedy cabbage
patches . . .*

*I*t's one thing for a reporter to ring you about your own press release, quite another to be approached unexpectedly over an issue you perhaps know nothing about. It does happen, though, and it's best to be ready for it.

Yes, you've been caught on the hop and you don't have a ready answer. Or you *have* got an answer, but you suspect that it will be so intemperate that you'll regret it later. What should you do?

The short answer is that you play for time, but there are right and wrong ways of going about it.

- Don't *(see page 8)* say 'No comment'
- Do say you'll ring back with a comment within a reasonable length of time. This will vary according to the media involved (a radio station coming up to bulletin time at one extreme, or a weekly paper several days from its deadline at the other), but you should try to make it snappy.
- Before you ring off, taking the reporter's name and telephone number, find out as much as you can about the story. You may have to brief someone else who's better placed to respond than you.
- Now work quickly to find the facts and, if necessary, to find that other person to comment. Make sure that any stand-in knows who to ring and by what time.
- Finally, ring the reporter back, either to give your side of the story or to tell him who will. You can't stop him running the story, but you can do your very best to ensure that it's not one-sided.

Stirring it up

Listen to this!

*U*sing the media for **campaigning** has become a sophisticated art in the hands of groups with plenty of cash and well-honed organisational skills. But you can play the game, too, at a humble local level - always remembering that you can't expect kid-glove treatment from the media. If they give you space in the newspaper and time on the airwaves it's because they like the story, not because they necessarily sympathise with your or your point of view.

Here's a true case history . . .

Richard A. was outraged to find that there was no water in his taps over a series of hot summer evenings. He rang the local water company and was told that because of an overuse of hosepipes by other customers there was insufficient pressure for the water to reach his house.

When the water engineers delivered some large, unwieldly containers of drinking water to see him through the drought, they mentioned that a man across the road had already written several letters to the company without any action being taken. The neighbour was a minor celebrity, and Richard A. persuaded him that they should make their protest public.

He sent a press release to the local paper, explaining that several households (including young families and elderly people living alone) were without water, and giving his neighbour's name and telephone number. Two days later the celebrity and his wife were pictured outside their cottage, struggling with one of the containers.

Events now moved swiftly. First the company was stung into a reply via a letter to the editor. Richard A. immediately proceeded to step two of his plan, writing a letter of his own which declared that this was a straightforward test case for a company which liked to parade concern for its customers: its integrity would be judged by the seriousness of its response.

Three days later he received a personal letter from a company spokesman, promising immediate short-term improvements and a long-term solution to the problem within a year. He passed this letter to the parish council, which agreed to keep the company to its promises.

Finally, he sent another letter to the local newspaper, congratulating the company on an effective response to their customers' complaints, and looking forward to the completion of the promised work. *It was done on time!*

Step-by-step . . .

1 Find a good angle for your story (the suffering of young and old/the celebrity)

2 Write a strong press release with reliable contact numbers

3 Keep the campaign on the boil (the letter to the editor/parish council involvement)

4 Establish publicly what has been promised (the gracious letter)

Headline - the cassette

Our friendly audio
tips prepare you for
that very first radio
interview . . .

Reading what to do is all very well, but our
Headline audio cassette lets you *hear* how it
should be done - and not done!

Swiftly putting any techno-phobia to flight, it
allows you to concentrate on putting yourself
across 'on air' confidently and effectively.

Our mini tutorial - which assumes that
you've never been inside a radio studio in your
life - covers everything from news clips and
magazine programmes to phone-ins.

As with this book, we've kept it simple and
we've kept it cheap: the Headline cassette costs
just £2.50.

Cheques to: Pomegranate Press, Church
Cottage, Westmeston, Sussex BN6 8RH

*Yes, of course you'll be horribly nervous the first time out. But **radio** makes a great impact - and the experience can be fun!*

Taking to the air

*L*ocal and community radio stations are everywhere today, and they're hungry for material to fill their airspace. This means that your chances of being asked to appear on a 'live' programme to promote yourself, your campaign, your organisation or your product have never been better.

Sometimes you'll be asked to take part on the telephone from the comfort of your own home. There's undoubtedly an appeal to this, but you'll find it more difficult to relate to the disembodied voice of the presenter than if you visit the radio studio.

You may be asked to turn up at an 'unattended' studio, which is usually a bare room with little but a chair, a telephone and a microphone, with simple instructions (if someone hasn't spirited them away) on how to contact the station and go 'on air'. This experience isn't recommended for beginners, who are likely to feel pretty nervous in any case: if it's inevitable, get there in plenty of time and take a friend along with you for moral support.

It's better by far to visit the radio station itself. Our HEADLINE cassette *(facing page)* takes you through the experience of being interviewed on the

radio, but here are a few points to bear in mind:

- When you agree to the interview, establish what form it will take (will it be one-to-one with the presenter or a round-table discussion?) and, roughly, how long it will last.

- Make yourself a few notes, but in headline form only, highlighting the points you want to get across.

- You may, if you're lucky, be given a cup of coffee when you arrive, but don't expect to discuss the programme with the presenter before the interview begins. It's common to be waved into the studio while a record is playing, to be asked to say a few words for 'level' and to find yourself under way without warning.

- If you suspect that the presenter lacks some vital information about yourself or your organisation, by all means pass him a piece of paper giving him the basic details: GRISELDA GRIMSHAW, TREASURER, RELATE, WORKSOP BRANCH. After that, leave it to him.

- Look the presenter in the eye and forget the audience outside. Relate only to him and the big wide world will look after itself.

- Speak naturally. Avoid jargon. Smile, when appropriate. Enjoy yourself!

When you're approached to give a radio interview it's important to establish what the

Radio lore

interviewer has in mind. You can't control the final product, but you need some idea of where your words will fit. Ask how long the interview will be ('live' or when edited), and what sort of programme it will go into. Don't expect to be told exactly what questions you'll be asked, but do find out which areas are to be covered. Here's a run-down of the possibilities:

News clips: Newsrooms use short inserts to pep up their bulletins. The maximum length is about 40 seconds, and interviews are often conducted over the telephone. The interviewer's voice is usually edited out, and parts of what you say may be pieced together to make a greater impact - so make what you have to say strong and punchy.

Sequence programmes: In the more relaxed format of a 'live' sequence or magazine programme you may have five or ten minutes to talk. The atmosphere is more relaxed, but it's just as important to make what you say interesting. A bored presenter may always decide to play another disc instead.

Wraps, packages: A radio journalist will often include a short clip in a report of his own. This is a 'wrap', and the clip is likely to be even briefer than when standing alone in a bulletin. Or he'll include selected parts in a scripted 'package'. Since his script tells the tale economically, he'll fillet your interview for vivid illustration. That means he'll chop out the boring bits.

News interviews: Whether 'live' or recorded, these will usually run for about three minutes at most. However strongly you feel that your subject is worth a good half an hour, only three minutes' worth will be heard on air. This should concentrate the mind.

Phone-ins: If you're a guest on a phone-in you'll be given headphones to wear, which can be a little offputting at first: do tell the presenter if you can't hear properly. Make sure that you have pen and paper to hand so that you can make a note of the callers' names and the gist of what they're saying. Talk to the callers, not about them through the presenter: 'That's an interesting point, Viv', rather than 'She's made an interesting point.' Ask the presenter beforehand what kind of pace he's after, so that you know whether to answer callers briefly or in more detail.

28

Worth a thousand words

*It may not make you a star, but you'll find that a **television** appearance can work wonders*

*I*f you find yourself invited to appear on the regional television station, the likelihood is that the camera will come to you. Be prepared for a lengthy session, because finding the right conditions for the camera and setting up all the equipment can take quite a time.

Be prepared, too, for feeling an insignificant cog in a large machine, however pleasant the reporter may be. Expect to be moved here and there in an experimental fashion, and to have your minutes of wisdom eventually distilled to perhaps thirty seconds on air - if you're lucky.

The positive to all these negatives, however, is that television does make a great impact *(see page 10)*, and that you'll probably find the necessary tribulations well worth while.

You'll find being interviewed in the television studio a different experience altogether - and different from the radio experience, too, although both demand a performance from you:

- Dress as seems appropriate, but note that bright white clothing and check or herringbone designs can cause some uncomfortable visual effects which may detract from what you have to say. Ask beforehand if you're in doubt.

- Don't be put off by the overpowering clutter of technology in the TV studio. It's there to serve a human purpose, after all, so concentrate on the people you meet, and forget the wiring.

- Once the interview starts, not only do the radio rules of speaking naturally and relating to the presenter come into play, but you have your 'body language' to consider, too. In all the excitement you probably won't notice what your limbs are doing, so it's best to decide beforehand which potentially annoying personal tics you'll avoid.

- Don't drop your guard. In a round-table discussion you may be happy to relax while other people have their say, but don't forget that there'll be more than one camera in use. While one has the speaker in close-up, the other may just be turned on you, waiting for a meaningful non-verbal reaction. *Oops!*

Did you take up our Newsbreaks challenge on page 2? There are no hard and fast answers in the headline-hunting game, but here are our suggested solutions . . .

Moments of truth

Newsbreak 1
Don't strangle the poor fellow - he's only doing his job, and it sounds a pretty dull one, too. He's probably desperate for 'copy', so why not tell him your exciting export news? Work it into the tax story somehow. (Won't you be paying more tax because you're doing so well?) And don't forget that you may need HIM one day.

Newsbreak 2
Pure cowardice if you accept. The reporter may, by the smallest chance, be interested, but there's no substitute for researching the local media for yourself and knowing who's who. Don't trust to chance: put yourself in charge!

Newsbreak 3
Don't risk repetitive strain injury. This is a typical victim-versus-oppressor case. All you need do is send a brief letter to the media, stating that because of the council's inhumane behaviour you're forced (saying when and where) to chain yourself to the railings outside the council offices/put your bed in the garden and lie on it for the cameras. The reporters will ask you all they need to know.

Newsbreak 4
Impossible! Don't delude yourself that those reporters have the slightest interest in chess. Just enjoy the limelight.

Newsbreak 5
Smile! You've some justification for feeling annoyed, but did you do your homework for this interview? Make the best of it and resolve to be better prepared next time. And make sure that you throw in the name of your pub once or twice.

Newsbreak 6
This is a political question, and we'll bounce the ball back into your court. If the Commodore's goodwill means everything to you, put him on. If you really care about the sailing club, don't let him near the camera. Find him something to be busy with when the crew arrives.